LEADERSHIP

Qualities and Importance.

Bhagyashree Kindre

Table of Contains

- Meaning of leader
- Responsibility of leader.
- Why a leader is Important.
- What are the qualities required in good leaders?
- What if leadership fails?
- What are things to take care of a good leader?
- Conclusion

LEADERSHIP
Qualities and Importance.

BHAGYASHREE KINDRE

Meaning of leader

Leadership is the art, knowledge, and skill of guiding a group of individuals toward a common goal or objective. A leader, in turn, is someone who assumes the responsibility of providing direction, making decisions, and motivating others to work collectively to achieve projected goals. Effective leadership is not solely about holding a position of authority; it encompasses a set of qualities, skills, and behaviors that inspire confidence and foster collaboration within a team or organization.

At its core, leadership involves the ability to envision a future, articulate that vision, and influence others to actively contribute toward its realization. A leader sets the course by providing a roadmap for success, ensuring that each team member understands their role and purpose in the collective journey.

Communication is a pivotal aspect of leadership. A leader must convey ideas clearly, listen actively to feedback, and foster an open and inclusive dialogue within the group. Effective communication builds trust and understanding, key components in creating a cohesive and motivated team.

Leadership also requires a judicious approach to decision-making. Leaders analyze situations, weigh options, and make informed choices that align with the overall objectives. Decisiveness, coupled with adaptability, is crucial in navigating the challenges and uncertainties that arise.

Empathy and emotional intelligence are traits that distinguish great leaders. Understanding the needs and perspectives of team members fosters a positive work environment. Leaders with high emotional intelligence can connect with others on a personal level, promoting collaboration and camaraderie.

In conclusion, leadership is a dynamic and multifaceted concept involving the ability to inspire, guide, and influence others towards a common goal. A leader embodies qualities such as vision, communication skills, decisiveness, and empathy. Successful leadership creates an environment where individuals feel empowered, valued, and motivated to contribute their best efforts toward shared objectives.

Responsibility of leader.

The responsibilities of a leader are diverse and multifaceted, encompassing various aspects of guiding and managing a team or organization. Here are key areas of responsibility for a leader:

Vision Setting:

Define Goals: Leaders articulate a clear vision and set specific, achievable goals for the team or organization.

Provide Direction: They establish the direction in which the team should move, aligning efforts toward a common purpose.

Decision-Making:

Make Informed Decisions: Leaders are responsible for making decisions that impact the team or organization, weighing options and considering the consequences.

Take Accountability: Good leaders take responsibility for the outcomes of their decisions, whether positive or negative.

Communication:

Effective Communication: Leaders must communicate clearly and transparently, ensuring that team members understand expectations, goals, and any changes in direction.

Active Listening: Listening to the concerns, ideas, and feedback of team members is crucial for building trust and understanding.

Team Building:

Recruitment and Development: Leaders play a role in recruiting the right talent and developing the skills of team members.

Foster Collaboration: They create an environment that encourages teamwork, cooperation, and open communication among team members.

Motivation and Inspiration:

Inspire Others: Leaders motivate and inspire their team members, instilling a sense of purpose and enthusiasm.

Recognition: Acknowledging and rewarding achievements fosters a positive and motivated work environment.

Problem-Solving:

Address Challenges: Leaders tackle problems and challenges that arise within the team or organization, seeking solutions and encouraging a proactive approach to issues.

Crisis Management: In times of crisis, leaders remain composed and guide the team through challenges.

Adaptability:

Navigate Change: Leaders adapt to changing circumstances, adjust strategies when needed, and guide the team through transitions.

Innovation: Encouraging innovation and a willingness to embrace new ideas contribute to long-term success.

Empowerment:

Delegate Authority: Leaders empower team members by entrusting them with responsibilities and authority.

Encourage Autonomy: Fostering a sense of ownership and autonomy among team members promotes a proactive and engaged workforce.

Ethical Leadership:

Model Integrity: Leaders set an example by adhering to ethical standards and displaying integrity in their actions.

Promote a Positive Culture: Creating a culture of trust and ethical behavior is essential for the long-term success of the team or organization.

Continuous Improvement:

Encourage Learning: Leaders support a culture of continuous learning and improvement, both individually and collectively.

Seek Feedback: They actively seek feedback from team members and use it to make adjustments and enhancements.

In summary, the responsibilities of a leader encompass a wide range of activities, from setting a vision and making decisions to fostering a positive team culture and promoting continuous improvement. Effective leadership involves a combination of strategic thinking, interpersonal skills, and a commitment to the success and well-being of the team or organization.

Why a leader is Important.

Leaders play a crucial role in any organization, community, or group due to the following reasons:

Guidance and Direction:

Leaders provide a sense of direction by setting goals and outlining the path to achieve them. Their vision and strategic planning help the group navigate challenges and work toward a common purpose.

Inspiration and Motivation:

Effective leaders inspire and motivate individuals within the group. Their enthusiasm and passion create a positive work environment, encouraging others to strive for excellence and contribute their best efforts.

Decision-Making:

Leaders are responsible for making informed decisions that impact the group. Their ability to weigh options, analyze situations, and make timely choices contributes to the effective functioning and progress of the organization.

Conflict Resolution:

Conflicts inevitably arise in any group setting. Leaders are essential in resolving disputes, fostering collaboration, and maintaining a harmonious atmosphere. Their guidance ensures that disagreements do not hinder overall productivity.

Accountability:

Leaders hold themselves and others accountable for their actions. This accountability helps establish a culture of responsibility and encourages individuals to meet their commitments and contribute to the group's success.

Communication:

Leaders facilitate effective communication within the group. They convey expectations, share information, and ensure that everyone is on the same page. Open and transparent communication is vital for building trust and cohesion.

Resource Management:

Leaders are responsible for managing resources, whether it be financial, human, or material. They allocate resources efficiently, ensuring that the group's needs are met while maintaining a focus on long-term sustainability.

Team Building:

Leaders foster a sense of unity and camaraderie among team members. They promote collaboration, build strong relationships, and create an inclusive environment where everyone feels valued and supported.

Adaptability:

In a rapidly changing world, leaders guide their teams through transitions and uncertainties. Their ability to adapt to new challenges, adjust strategies, and lead with resilience is crucial for the group's survival and growth.

Innovation and Creativity:

Leaders encourage a culture of innovation and creativity. They inspire individuals to think outside the box, explore new ideas, and contribute to the organization's evolution and competitiveness.

Long-Term Vision:

Leaders have a long-term vision for the group's success. They provide stability by focusing on the bigger picture, setting strategic goals, and steering the organization toward sustained growth and achievement.

In essence, leaders are important because they provide guidance, motivation, and direction to a group. Their influence extends to various aspects of organizational life, contributing to productivity, harmony, and the overall success of the group. Effective leadership is a driving force that shapes the culture, values, and outcomes of any collective endeavor.

What are the qualities required in good leaders?

Effective leaders possess a diverse set of qualities that enable them to navigate challenges, inspire others, and drive success. Here are some key qualities required in good leaders:

Vision:

Good leaders have a clear vision of the future and can communicate it in a way that inspires and motivates others. They provide a sense of direction and purpose.

Integrity:

Leaders with integrity gain trust and respect. They adhere to ethical principles, are honest, and consistently demonstrate moral and ethical behavior.

Empathy:

Empathetic leaders understand and relate to the feelings and perspectives of others. They build strong connections, creating a positive and supportive work environment.

Communication Skills:

Effective communication is crucial. Leaders articulate ideas clearly, listen actively, and ensure that information is conveyed in a way that is easily understood by the team.

Decisiveness:

Leaders make timely and informed decisions. They weigh options, consider the consequences, and take decisive actions, providing a sense of direction to the team.

Adaptability:

In a dynamic world, leaders must be adaptable. They navigate change with resilience, adjusting strategies and approaches to meet evolving challenges.

Confidence:

Confidence instills trust in the team. Leaders project self-assurance, inspiring others to believe in the vision and goals set by the organization.

Inspirational:

Inspirational leaders motivate and uplift their team. They foster a sense of enthusiasm and commitment, encouraging individuals to go above and beyond.

Accountability:

Good leaders take responsibility for their actions and decisions. They hold themselves and their team members accountable, fostering a culture of responsibility.

Strategic Thinking:

Leaders think strategically, considering the long-term impact of decisions. They analyze situations, anticipate challenges, and plan for the future success of the organization.

Resilience:

Resilient leaders bounce back from setbacks. They face challenges with composure, learn from experiences, and maintain a positive outlook during difficult times.

Team-Oriented:

Leaders prioritize teamwork and collaboration. They build a sense of unity within the team, recognizing that collective efforts lead to greater success.

Open-Mindedness:

Open-minded leaders are receptive to new ideas and perspectives. They encourage innovation and create a culture where diverse thoughts and opinions are valued.

Courage:

Courageous leaders take calculated risks and confront challenges head-on. They stand firm in their convictions and make tough decisions when necessary.

Humility:

Humble leaders acknowledge the contributions of others and are open to learning. They do not seek personal glory but focus on the collective success of the team.

Strive for Excellence:

Leaders set high standards for themselves and their team. They inspire a commitment to excellence, encouraging continuous improvement and growth.

Delegation:

Effective leaders delegate tasks and responsibilities. They empower team members, recognizing and utilizing individual strengths for the overall benefit of the organization.

Time Management:

Leaders prioritize tasks effectively, demonstrating good time management skills. This ensures that resources are utilized efficiently and goals are achieved within set timelines.

These qualities are not exhaustive, and the ideal combination may vary depending on the specific context and challenges faced by a leader. However, possessing a mix of these qualities can contribute to effective and impactful leadership.

What if leadership fails?

Leadership can fail for various reasons, and the consequences of leadership failure can have significant impacts on individuals, teams, and organizations. Here are some potential outcomes when leadership fails:

Loss of Trust:

One of the most critical consequences of leadership failure is the erosion of trust. When leaders fail to uphold ethical standards, make poor decisions, or display inconsistency, trust among team members can be damaged or lost.

Decreased Morale:

Leadership failure can lead to a decline in morale among team members. When individuals perceive a lack of direction, integrity, or competence from their leaders, it can negatively affect their motivation and job satisfaction.

Increased Turnover:

Employees may choose to leave an organization with ineffective leadership. High turnover can disrupt team dynamics, impact productivity, and result in the loss of valuable talent.

Poor Performance:

A lack of effective leadership can contribute to poor organizational performance. Without clear direction, motivation, and support, teams may struggle to meet goals and objectives, hindering overall success.

Resistance to Change:

Leadership failure may create an environment where individuals resist change initiatives. Without confidence in leadership, employees may be skeptical of new strategies or directions proposed by the leadership team.

Communication Breakdown:

Failed leadership often leads to communication breakdowns. If leaders are not transparent, open, or effective in conveying information, misinformation or lack of information can spread, causing confusion and uncertainty.

Lack of Innovation:

Effective leaders foster innovation by encouraging creativity and risk-taking. When leadership fails, there may be a reluctance to explore new ideas, stifling innovation and hindering the organization's ability to adapt to changing circumstances.

Legal and Ethical Issues:

Leadership failure can sometimes result in legal and ethical challenges. Poor decision-making, lack of adherence to regulations, or unethical behavior by leaders may expose the organization to legal consequences and damage its reputation.

Crisis Management Challenges:

In times of crisis, effective leadership is crucial. Leadership failure may result in inadequate crisis management, exacerbating the impact of the crisis and prolonging recovery efforts.

Negative Organizational Culture:

Leadership sets the tone for organizational culture. When leadership fails, it can contribute to a negative culture characterized by distrust, fear, and low morale, which further hinders the organization's overall effectiveness.

Reputation Damage:

Leadership failure can harm the organization's reputation both internally and externally. A damaged reputation can affect relationships with customers, partners, and other stakeholders.

It's important to note that leadership failure is not irreversible. Organizations can take steps to address and rectify leadership issues. This may involve leadership development, coaching, changes in leadership personnel, or a comprehensive review and restructuring of organizational processes. Recognizing and addressing leadership failures proactively is key to minimizing negative impacts and fostering a healthier and more successful organizational environment.

What are things to take care of a good leader?

To be a good leader, there are several key things to take care of. These aspects encompass personal development, effective communication, relationship building, and a focus on the well-being of the team. Here are some crucial elements for a good leader to consider:

Self-Development:

Continuous Learning: A good leader is committed to ongoing self-improvement. This includes staying updated on industry trends, acquiring new skills, and seeking knowledge to enhance leadership capabilities.

Effective Communication:

Clear and Transparent Communication: A good leader communicates clearly, ensuring that team members understand goals, expectations, and changes. Transparent communication builds trust and fosters a positive work environment.

Vision and Direction:

Set a Clear Vision: A good leader establishes a compelling vision for the team or organization. Communicate this vision to inspire and guide team members towards common goals.

Empathy:

Understanding Team Members: Good leaders practice empathy by understanding the perspectives, concerns, and needs of their team members. This helps build strong relationships and a supportive team culture.

Decision-Making:

Informed Decision-Making: A good leader makes informed decisions based on thorough analysis and consideration of various factors. They take responsibility for the outcomes of their decisions.

Delegation:

Empower Team Members: Delegating tasks and responsibilities empowers team members. A good leader trusts their team, recognizes individual strengths, and encourages autonomy.

Motivation:

Inspire and Motivate: Good leaders inspire and motivate their team through positive reinforcement, recognition of achievements, and creating a work environment that fosters enthusiasm.

Conflict Resolution:

Address Conflicts Proactively: Conflict is inevitable, but a good leader addresses conflicts promptly and proactively. This involves active listening, understanding different perspectives, and finding constructive solutions.

Accountability:

Lead by Example: Good leaders set high standards for themselves and lead by example. They hold themselves and their team members accountable for their actions and commitments.

Adaptability:

Adapt to Change: In a dynamic environment, a good leader is adaptable. They navigate change with resilience, adjust strategies when needed, and guide the team through transitions.

Team Building:

Foster Team Collaboration: Building a cohesive team is essential. A good leader fosters collaboration, encourages open communication, and creates a sense of unity among team members.

Recognition:

Acknowledge Achievements: Recognizing and celebrating individual and team achievements reinforces positive behavior and motivates continued excellence.

Well-Being:

Consider Team Well-Being: A good leader cares about the well-being of their team members. This includes promoting work-life balance, addressing stressors, and creating a supportive work environment.

Feedback:

Provide Constructive Feedback: Regular feedback helps team members grow. A good leader provides constructive feedback, highlighting strengths and areas for improvement.

Strategic Thinking:

Focus on the Big Picture: Good leaders think strategically. They consider the long-term goals of the organization, make decisions aligned with the overall strategy, and guide the team towards

sustained success.

By focusing on these elements, a good leader can create a positive and productive work environment, foster a motivated and engaged team, and contribute to the overall success of the organization.

Additional Leadership qualities

Futuristic Vision:

Possesses the ability to envision and plan for the future, guiding the team toward long-term goals.

Holistic Decision-Making:

Considers the broader implications and interconnectedness of decisions, taking into account the impact on various aspects of the organization.

Interpersonal Sensitivity:

Demonstrates a keen understanding of others' emotions and perspectives, promoting positive relationships.

Situational Awareness:

Stays attentive to the current context, adapting leadership styles and decisions based on the specific situation.

Ho acracy:

Embraces a non-hierarchical organizational structure that distributes authority, fostering a more collaborative and flexible work environment.

Wellness Advocate:

Prioritizes and promotes the physical and mental well-being of team members, recognizing its impact on performance.

Generational Inclusivity:

Values and incorporates the diverse strengths and perspectives of individuals from different age groups within the team.

Adaptive Leadership:

Adjusts leadership approaches based on changing circumstances, ensuring resilience and responsiveness.

Collaborative Innovation:

Encourages and facilitates teamwork in generating new ideas and solutions through collaborative innovation.

Purpose-Driven:

Aligns actions and decisions with a sense of purpose, inspiring a shared commitment to meaningful goals.

Digital Literacy:

Possesses proficiency in utilizing and leveraging digital tools and technologies to enhance organizational efficiency.

Data-Driven Decision-Making:

Relies on data and analytics to inform and support decision-making processes for more effective outcomes.

Empathetic Decision-Making:

Considers the impact of decisions on individuals, demonstrating empathy and understanding.

Responsible Risk-Taking:

Takes calculated risks while considering potential consequences, fostering a culture of innovation.

Cross-Cultural Competence:

Navigates and respects cultural differences, promoting inclusivity and collaboration in a globalized world.

Narrative Leadership:

Uses storytelling as a powerful tool to communicate values, inspire, and create a shared sense of purpose.

Integrity Champion:

Upholds strong moral and ethical principles, acting with honesty and transparency.

Mindfulness Practices:

Incorporates mindfulness techniques to enhance focus, resilience, and overall well-being.

Empowerment Catalyst:

Actively supports and enables individuals to reach their full potential, fostering empowerment and growth.

Community Builder:

Engages in community-building initiatives, contributing to positive relationships beyond the organization.

Innovative Thinking:

Cultivates a culture of creativity and innovative thinking, encouraging novel approaches to problem-solving.

Boundaryless Leadership:

Transcends traditional organizational boundaries, promoting collaboration and information sharing.

Conflict Prevention:

Proactively addresses potential conflicts before they escalate, maintaining a harmonious work environment.

Emotional Intelligence:

Demonstrates a high level of emotional intelligence, understanding and managing personal emotions and those of others.

Systems Thinking:

Considers the organization as a complex system, understanding the interdependence of its components.

Balanced Feedback:

Provides a balanced mix of positive and constructive feedback, promoting continuous improvement without demotivating.

Digital Transformation Advocate:

Drives and supports the organization's digital transformation, embracing technological advancements.

Holistic Leadership Development:

Invests in comprehensive leadership development programs that address various aspects of leadership skills and qualities.

Gratitude Practices:

Expresses gratitude and appreciation, fostering a positive and inclusive organizational culture.

Decentralized Decision-Making:

Empowers team members to make decisions independently, fostering a sense of responsibility and autonomy.

Environmental Consciousness:

Demonstrates a commitment to sustainable and environmentally friendly practices, aligning leadership with broader social responsibilities.

Negotiation Skills:

Effectively navigates and resolves conflicts through negotiation, finding mutually beneficial solutions.

Global Awareness:

Possesses a broad understanding of global trends and issues, enabling informed decision-making in a global context.

Open-Door Policy:

Encourages an open-door communication approach, making leaders accessible to team members for discussions and feedback.

Time Management:

Efficiently prioritizes tasks and allocates time to maximize productivity and meet deadlines.

Strategic Networking:

Cultivates valuable professional relationships to leverage networks for the benefit of the team or organization.

Proactive Problem Solver:

Identifies potential issues early on and takes proactive measures to prevent or address them before they escalate.

Team Empowerment:

Actively involves and empowers team members, recognizing and utilizing their strengths for collective success.

Cultural Competence:

Understands and appreciates diverse cultures, adapting leadership approaches to be inclusive and culturally sensitive.

Continuous Improvement Advocate:

Promotes a culture of constant learning and improvement, encouraging the team to seek better ways of doing things.

Resourcefulness:

Effectively utilizes available resources, demonstrating creativity and adaptability in overcoming challenges.

Feedback Receptivity:

Welcomes and values constructive feedback, using it as a tool for personal and professional development.

Cross-Functional Collaboration:

Encourages collaboration across different departments or functions, fostering a holistic and integrated approach to problem-solving.

Holistic Thinker:

Considers the interconnectedness of various factors when making decisions, avoiding siloed perspectives.

Learning Agility:

Quickly adapts and learns in new situations, demonstrating agility in acquiring new skills and knowledge.

Emotional Resonance:

Connects with team members on an emotional level, creating a positive and supportive work environment.

Conflict Transformation:

Transforms conflicts into opportunities for growth and improvement, rather than allowing them to escalate negatively.

Succession Planning:

Plans for the long-term by identifying and developing potential future leaders within the organization.

Storytelling Skills:

Effectively communicates messages and values through compelling and relatable stories.

Community Engagement:

Actively participates in and contributes to the local or broader community, aligning leadership with social responsibility.

Conclusion

In conclusion, leadership is about guiding and inspiring a group of people to work together toward a common goal. A good leader sets a clear direction, communicates effectively, and cares about the well-being of the team. Leadership involves making wise decisions, fostering a positive environment, and helping others grow. Whether in a workplace, community, or any group, strong leadership is key to achieving success and creating a supportive and thriving atmosphere for everyone involved.